I0407894

Extreme Coloring Book

Copyright: Published in the United States by Peter Raymond
Published April 2017
ISBN-13: 978-1545314326
ISBN-10: 1545314322

Thank you

www.ingramcontent.com/pod-product-compliance
Lightning Source LLC
Chambersburg PA
CBHW081555280526
45788CB00011B/3475